A word from the author

I have been working alongside teenage refugees since I
moved to Norway over 7 years ago, and in this time I have
met I000s of teenagers from many different countries, each
with their own story to tell. What some of these kids have
gone through is horrendous, how they have the strength to
carry on, inspiring.

But there is a clear disparity between the children I have
had the privelege of working with, and how they are
portrayed in the media, and perceived in general. Their
individual stories were reduced to numbers and statistics
in news reports, and most of the coverage appeared
negative- focusing on problems that may arise as a result
of increased immigration, as opposed to the problems that
the refugees themselves face, and the horrors they may have
endured, not only in the countries that they come from, on
their journey to a new country, but also after they arrive
at their destination.

I wanted to give these children a voice, to give children
in Norway a glimpse of what some of these kids go through.
I wanted to inspire discussions around these issues, and to
hopefully give young people a better understanding of
refugees.

This is a true story.

It is one of many.

My Name is Yemane

My name is Yemane. I'm I7 years old.

I left home at I5, and in the same moment left
behind my family, my friends, my country, and
everything that I knew.

I come from a country called Eritrea, in
Eastern Africa. It is a beautiful land with
amazing people, food, nature, wildlife.

I love my country.

Someone once told me that Eritreans have music
in their soul.

But it is also a land riddled with corruption, war, and a government that sacrifices its own people to line their pockets.

It is not a safe country to live in, and, for a young teenager like myself, there is no future here. Soon I would be forced to become a soldier, and fight in a war that was not my own.

My family didn't want this for me. No one would
want this for their children. So like many
others, they scraped together money so that I
could escape, leave this land, and seek refuge
in Europe.

There I would be safe. I would be free. I could
live a normal life. I would have a future.

I didn't want to leave.

If the situation was different, if we had
democracy, if we had peace, then I would never
leave, but to stay was a death sentence.

My family made the hardest decision of their
lives that day, but one made out of love, with
hope that their child would be safe.
They paid some people to smuggle me to Europe.
First, I would go to Libya, where I would get a
boat across the sea to Europe. There I would be
safe.

The day came that I had to say goodbye to my family. Leaving was both full of hope and full of sadness. I knew that I would most likely never see them again.
I still cry each day when I think of my family.

I had heard stories of Libya, and knew that it
was a bad place, but nothing could prepare me
for what I encountered.
Young refugees like me were locked up, chained,
forced to work, beaten, starved.
It was a nightmare.

For others, it was much worse.

The people in charge demanded more money for me
to carry on my journey. My family had already
paid. But that didn't matter. They would have
to pay more, or I would be forced to stay here.
Some would never leave.

My family paid.

Beaten, bruised, and scarred, I was one of the
lucky ones.

The day came when I was told that it was my turn to take a boat and continue my journey to Europe. A large group of us- boys, girls, mothers, and their babies were hustled into a lorry that took us to the boat.

This old boat may have looked dirty, unsafe,
and unfit for anything more than scrap, but to
us who were about to board, it was the most
beautiful thing that we had ever seen.
It represented hope, freedom, and would not
just be carrying us across the sea, but our
dreams.
This was it. Our next destination was Europe.
Soon the horrors of Libya, and whatever the
seas had to throw at us, would be behind us.

If only it were that easy.

The boat was more than just overcrowded. We sat
huddled, holding one another as the waves
crashed around us. Mothers clung to their
children. No one spoke. The only sounds aboard
were of tears, and mothers trying to soothe
their children.

Everyone was scared. As we clung on to each
other, we were also clinging on to hope of what
tomorrow may bring.

Several hours in, our boat ran into trouble. At
first we did not know what was happening, but
then saw the smoke coming from within. There
was a fire.

Many of us, including myself, could not swim.
It was a choice between burning or drowning. We
had to jump off the boat to survive- holding on
to anything we could find that would float.
I thought I would die right there and then, and
as I clung on, I thought I was just prolonging
the inevitable.

But that was not God's plan. A passing boat,
drawn by the plumes of smoke, found us.
Amazingly, everyone survived.
The boat took us to an island called Malta.
Here I thought I would be safe. A beautiful
island with beaches, sunshine, and bustling
with tourists.

But for us refugees, Malta was as bad as Lybia.

Again I was lucky. My family had money and were able to pay for someone to smuggle me to another country. I wonder if "lucky" is the right word. No one who was lucky would have to endure these horrors. But I was lucky to escape them.

I was given a fake passport, boarded a plane, and finally, several months after saying goodbye to my family, friends, and everything that I knew, I arrived in Norway.

ere for the first time, I was met with warmth;
with smiles, and people treated me like a human
being.
I found a home, albeit temporary, in a camp,
where I met others like me- from Syria,
Afghanistan, Sudan and Ukraine, to name just a
few of the countries the others came from.

I found friendship, and happiness.

I managed to smile.

I had hope.

But every night in my room I would cry. I cried
for my family, for everything I had lost, for
everything I had endured. I cried for those
that would never make it.
I knew that I would always be sad inside, but
maybe one day I would find true happiness and a
forever home...

A new life here in Norway.

The days passed, rolling into weeks, then months. I went to school, started to learn Norwegian, and I slowly found myself relaxing , as I waited for the government to process my application.

Then one day, the phone rang. It was a lawyer.
I was going to be deported to Malta.

Norway, this country that had been so kind to
me, was sending me back, even though they knew
what I had been through. Why would they do this
to a child? How could they do this to me?
I would rather die than go back there.
So I packed my bag and ran.

I had no idea where I was going, or what I'd
need to do to survive.

But I still had hope.

Some Notes about Asylum

What is an Asylum Seeker?

An asylum seeker is someone who has been forced to leave
their country, and seeks protection and the right to live in
another country. Once they have been granted asylum in that
country they are then reclassified as a refugee.

Grounds for Applying for Asylum

Someone can apply for asylum if their life and freedom are
in danger in their homecountry because of their:
- race
- nationality
- religion
- membership of a special social group
- political beliefs
- because of the security situation in their country, for
  example in the case of war
- or if they are at risk of the death penalty or torture
  should they return to their home country.

A person may also be granted asylum on humanitarian grounds
in the case of a serious health condition, where treatment
is unavailable in their homecountry.

A person cannot apply for asylum if they are merely coming
here to work, study, or be with family members. These are
different forms of migration, each with their own rules and
regulations. Likewise, a poor economic situation in a
persons home country is not enough grounds for asylum.

Unaccompanied Asylum Seeking Children (UASC)

An unaccompanied asylum seeking child, is someone below the age of I8, who arrives in a country to seek asylum, without their parents or carers present.

The Number of Asylum Seekers to Europe and Norway

The number of people seeking asylum in Europe has increased considerably in the last decade and whilst the totals can vary greatly, has been over 400,000 each year since 20I4, reaching highs of over I million in 20I5 and 20I6 (eurostat). Of these around I0% are unaccompanied minors. Norway has had between between I386 and 3560 asylum applications each year between 20I6 and 202I. However there were over 30,000 applications made in 20I5 (UDI).

In 2022 there were over 4,500 applications mere made in Norway with over I000 these coming from unaccompanied minors. Approximately half of the applications made came from refugees from Ukraine (UDI).

The Need for ID

Alongside having grounds for applying for asylum, asylum seekers need to also provide proof of who they are, normally in the form of some form of accepted ID, such as a passport. Many asylum seekers are unable to provide documention, either because they have never had any, are unable to obtain it from their homecountry, or the documents have either been take from them, or lost, on their journey. Without valid ID, an asylum application can be denied, or protection may be granted but only for a limited time. This can have drastic consequences for an asylum seeker.

What Happens after Applying

After applying for asylum in Norway, an asylum seeker is sent to a camp, where they will be given information, health checks, food, and, in some cases, some basic schooling. Here they will normally wait until they are given an asylum interview, before being transferred to another camp to await the decision on their application. If successful they will be offered a place to live somewhere within Norway. This process takes on average 4-8 months, but in some cases asylum seekers can be waiting much longer.

The Dublin Regulation

The Dublin Regulation is an agreement between the EU countries, and Iceland, Switzerland, Liechtenstein and Norway, that an asylum seeker should apply for asylum in the first safe country that they arrive in, and should not travel further. If they travel further after being documented in any country that is part of this agreement, they risk being returned to the initial country that they were documented in.

There are many reason why asylum seekers choose to move on to another country- these can include the first country not having the resources to provide for the number of refugees arriving, as is the case in Greece, abuse at the hands of the authorities in some countries, or having family members living in another country to the one they initially arrive in.

If an asylum seeker who is a "dubliner" arrives in Norway, and are deemed to be under 18 years of age, there is a chance that their case will be handled in Norway, instead of them being returned to another country.

Age Testing

In Norway, the majority asylum seekers between the ages of
I5 and I8 are age-tested. This involves an x-ray of their
teeth, which specialists use to determine the likelihood
that a person is a certain age. In the absence of any
accepted forms of ID, it this this test that will determine
how old the UDI deem an asylum seeker to be. Opinions on
this form of testing are very divided, with much criticism
being directed at the accuracy of this form of testing.

The Importance of Age

What the UDI deem a persons age to be can impact an asylum
seeker in many different areas. If they are a "dubliner", it
can mean the difference between having their claim processed
here in Norway, or being returned to another country. It can
affect an asylum seekers rights to have their family join
them in Norway. It can affect what education and other
benefits the asylum seeker is entitled to. It can even
result in an asylum seeker being deported to their home
country.

Family Reunification

Sadly many asylum seekers will never see their family again.
However, if an asylum seeker's application is successful,
and they are under the age of I8 when they are granted
asylum, their close family, such as parents and and siblings
may be able to apply to join them in Norway,

Returns and Deportation

In the case of a failed asylum application, an asylum seeker
can complain and have their case reassessed. If after this
process, they are still not granted asylum, then they can
either leave Norway themselves, or apply for help to return
voluntarily to their home country.

If they refuse to leave, either by their own hand, or with
assistance, they can be forcibly returned, and risk being
imprisoned until their deportation. In the case of a forced
return, an asylum seeker is not allowed to return to any
Schengen country for a period of I-5 years, and they must
cover all the costs of deportation, such as the flights,
themselves.

Some failed asylum seekers under the age of I8 are allowed
to remain until they turn I8, and are then forcibly
returned.

It is well documented that many failed asylum seekers have
fled Norway, and sought asylum elsewhere. Despite being
classed as "dubliners", other countries have assessed their
cases more favourably and granted them asylum.

And others simply vanish. A report by the UDI found that up
to I in 5 asylum seekers had left reception centres and were
reported as missing. Some were later found by authorities-
afterwards choosing to leave Norway voluntarily. Some were
forcibly returned to their homecountry. A small number were
granted asylum.

The vast majority remain unaccounted for.

Thanks

I would like to express my heartfelt gratitude to the following organizations for their unwavering support and invaluable feedback throughout the creation of this book. Their exceptional work on behalf of refugees has been a constant source of inspiration and motivation:

Dråpen i havet

moriabevegelsen

First edition published July 2023
Text by Paul Wennersberg-Løvholen
Cover and illustrations by Paul Wennersberg-Løvholen

ISBN: 978-82-93748-33-5 (Hardback)
ISBN: 978-82-93748-34-2 (Paperback)
ISBN: 978-82-93748-35-9 (Kindle)

This book is also available in Norwegian:

Mitt Navn er Yemane

ISBN: 978-82-93748-36-6 (Hardback)
ISBN: 978-82-93748-37-3 (Paperback)
ISBN: 978-82-93748-38-0 (Kindle)

Published by Paul's Books, Eidsberg, Norway
fb.me/superfartypants